Bobcat Colouring Books for Charity

Wolves

Bobcat Colouring Books for Charity is proud to present Wolves a 30-page greyscale book for Wolf lovers worldwide.

The Wolf has been the villain of stories and fairy tales for many years, but this very sociable and extremely intelligent animal has done very little to gain this terrifying reputation.

Wolves are pack animals and partner for life, having up to six puppies per litter. Wolves have very strong relationships and together as a pack they are very strong. Wolves may even give their own life to protect their family and pack. They are mystical animals and creatures that legends are made of.

Wolves is a book in the Bobcat stable, of which the proceeds (after expenses) will be donated to no kill animal sanctuaries in South Africa, who are in desperate need of funds.

Images for this book were compiled by Carol Meikle.

Contact us:
carol.meikle@gmail.com
On Facebook: @BobcatColouringBooksForCharity
https://www.facebook.com/groups/500281364057343/

Made in the USA
Monee, IL
07 May 2021